请你不要这样做

Social Emotional and Multicultural Learning | Non-Fiction Series

Copyright © 2022 by Level Learning, INC. and Washington Yu Ying PCS™
Original and Edited Text Copyright © 2022 by Washington Yu Ying PCS™

All rights reserved. No part of this book in whole or part may be reproduced without written permission from the publisher.

Published by Level Learning, INC.

Content Contributors:
Washington Yu Ying PCS™
Level Learning - Ya-Ching Chang

Illustrations by: Josh Taira

Leveling classification based on Level Learning standard. For full description, visit www.levellearning.com

ISBN 978-1-64040-075-7
Simplified Chinese Edition

About Level Learning:

Level Learning provides a literacy focused curriculum specifically designed for K-12 Chinese as a Second Language classrooms. Our program offers 20 levels of specific and detailed objectives, leveled texts and passages, mastery-based online assessment, and analytics to enable data-driven instruction. Level Learning reading curriculum for both literature and informational text emphasize grammar and comprehension skills to help teachers develop confident and independent Chinese language readers. The non-fiction series of books are specifically designed to support our informational text course based on multiple national standards. To learn more about our entire offering, visit www.levellearning.com.

About Washington Yu Ying PCS™:

Washington Yu Ying PCS is a Mandarin English dual language immersion International Baccalaureate (IB) World school. Yu Ying's mission is to inspire and prepare young people to create a better world by challenging them to reach their full potential in a nurturing Chinese/English educational environment. Yu Ying's comprehensive IB, dual immersion curriculum equips students with global competencies for success in the real world. As a leader in immersion education, Yu Ying is determined to advance Chinese language programs and global citizenry education by helping other schools create and strengthen their Chinese programs. For more information, email: products@washingtonyuying.org

在学校你被人欺负过吗？别人欺负你的时候，你会怎么做呢？

有人推你或者打你。你觉得很害怕,你会怎么做?

我会告诉他,请你不要这样做。

有人抢你的东西。你觉得很生气，你会怎么做？

我会告诉他,请你不要这样做。

有人取笑你。你觉得不开心，你会怎么做？

我会告诉他，请你不要这样做。

有人说你的坏话。你觉得很难过,你会怎么做?

我会告诉他,请你不要这样做。

我会大声说出我的感受。

我不喜欢你这样做。

我还会告诉老师或朋友。

Glossary

	Pinyin	English Definition
欺负	qī fu	to bully
推	tuī	to push
打	dǎ	to hit, to beat, to fight
觉得	jué de	to feel
害怕	hài pà	to be afraid
怎么	zěn me	how
告诉	gào su	to tell
抢	qiǎng	to grab
生气	shēng qì	angry
取笑	qǔ xiào	make fun of
开心	kāi xīn	happy
坏话	huài huà	gossip
难过	nán guò	sad

	Pinyin	English Definition
大声	dà shēng	loudly
感受	gǎn shòu	to feel, to experience
还会	hái huì	will also
或	huò	or

www.ingramcontent.com/pod-product-compliance
Lightning Source LLC
Chambersburg PA
CBHW041220070526
44584CB00001B/30